Little People, BIG DREAMS™
STEVEN SPIELBERG

Written by
Maria Isabel Sánchez Vegara

Illustrated by
Keith Negley

Frances Lincoln
Children's Books

Little Steven was a quiet boy from Ohio who grew up in a family that enjoyed exploring their favorite things. His dad liked computers, and his mom, art. Steven wasn't sure what he loved most, but that was OK—he had time to find out!

As the movie ended, Steven knew in his heart that he wanted to be a filmmaker! The first scene he ever made was of a toy-train crash, inspired by the movie he saw that day.

Later, the family moved to Arizona. At his new school, kids teased Steven for being Jewish. To cope, he poured his energy into making a movie about cowboys with his friends and family. He wrote, filmed, and edited it all himself.

For his next short film, Steven asked his classmates to act in a big battle. He even got one of his bullies to play a hero. Making this choice helped him feel stronger. Finally, Steven was the one in charge!

At seventeen, Steven found a sneaky way into Universal Studios, where movies and TV shows were created. As he spent the summer exploring sets, asking questions, and watching real directors work, he realized he had found the place he truly belonged.

When his parents divorced, Steven felt very sad. This tough time would inspire many of his future movies. But first, he made a short film that earned him a job at Universal as the youngest director at a major Hollywood studio.

After proving himself by working on several TV movies, Steven got the chance to direct Jaws, the story of a giant shark.

Its huge success changed his life. From then on, he could choose the movies he wanted to make!

Steven decided to work on a movie inspired by his love and wonder for stars and space. It mixed science fiction with a heartfelt story about visitors from another planet. But his most beloved alien friend was still to be born . . .

People all over the world fell in love with *E.T.* This beautiful story of friendship between a lonely boy and a gentle alien turned Steven's childhood memories into something magical. And it helped others feel a little less lonely, too.

Later, Steven made history by using computers to bring dinosaurs to life. Before this, most creatures in movies were made with models or costumes. But even though he loved sci-fi, Steven knew there was a true story he needed to tell.

Schindler's List was about a man who saved many Jewish people during a terrible time in history. After the film was released, Steven created a foundation to make sure future generations could hear and remember the survivors' stories.

For decades, his films amazed audiences! Steven also gave filmmakers a chance to start their careers through Amblin, a company named after the short film that got him his first job. Later, he cofounded a major studio called DreamWorks.

And if you ever feel alone, or need a touch of magic, remember that little Steven's movies are always there, ready to guide you and fill your world with wonder.

STEVEN SPIELBERG

(Born 1946)

1978

1982

Steven Allan Spielberg was born in Ohio but moved to New Jersey before his family settled in Arizona in 1957. After a trip to the movies to see a film called *The Greatest Show on Earth*, he was inspired. He started making his own homemade films and visited the cinema as much as he could. At school, Steven faced anti-semitism because of his Jewish heritage. To find comfort, he channeled his energy into creating short films with his classmates. Later, Steven took a tour at Universal Studios and watched filmmakers at work. He wanted to explore the studios alone . . . so he hid in a bathroom until the rest of the tourists left without him! Luckily, an employee gave him a three-day pass, and this led to Steven becoming an unofficial apprentice at Universal Studios for the summer. After he made his

1999   2024

filmmaking debut in 1969, his career quickly took off. Steven went on to write and direct some of the world's most loved films, like *Jaws*, *E.T.*, *Indiana Jones*, *Saving Private Ryan,* and *Jurassic Park*. In 2022, he released *The Fabelmans,* a film based on his own childhood. Steven's hard work has won him many awards, including Academy Awards, Golden Globe Awards, and BAFTA Awards. He founded Amblin, his very own film studio. He also cofounded a film studio called DreamWorks that created some iconic movies, including *Shrek, How to Train Your Dragon,* and *Kung Fu Panda*. Throughout his career, Steven has kept experimenting and working with different art forms, including video games and theater shows. Today, Steven is considered to be one of the greatest filmmakers of all time.

Want to find out more about **Steven Spielberg**?

Have a read of this great book:

Steven Spielberg: A Little Golden Book Biography by Geof Smith

With an adult, you can watch some of Steven's films, like *E.T.*

To my friend Bram, a journey awaits you!

Text © 2025 Maria Isabel Sánchez Vegara. Illustrations © 2025 Keith Negley.
Original idea of the series by Maria Isabel Sánchez Vegara, published by Alba Editorial, s.l.u.
"Little People, BIG DREAMS" and "Pequeña & Grande" are trademarks of
Alba Editorial S.L.U. and/or Beautifool Couple S.L.
First published in the US in 2025 by Frances Lincoln Children's Books, an imprint of The Quarto Group.
Quarto Boston North Shore, 100 Cummings Center, Suite 265D, Beverly, MA 01915, USA
Tel: +1 978-282-9590 www.Quarto.com
EEA Representation, WTS Tax d.o.o., Žanova ulica 3, 4000 Kranj, Slovenia. www.wts-tax.si

No part of this publication may be reproduced, stored in a retrieval system, or transmitted, in any form, or by any means, electrical, mechanical, photocopying, recording, or otherwise without the prior written permission of the publisher or a license permitting restricted copying.

This book is not authorized, licensed, or approved by Steven Spielberg.
Any faults are the publisher's who will be happy to rectify for future printings.
ISBN 978-1-83600-746-3
Set in Futura BT.
Published by Peter Marley · Edited by Molly Mead
Designed by Sasha Moxon and Izzy Bowman
Production by Robin Boothroyd
Manufactured in Guangdong, China CC062025
1 3 5 7 9 8 6 4 2

Photographic acknowledgments (pages 28-29, from left to right): 1. American director, producer, and screenwriter Steven Spielberg, September 8, 1978. (Photo by Graham Morris/Evening Standard/Getty Images) 2. Director Steven Spielberg poses with E.T. at Carlo Rimbaldi studio in April 1982 in Los Angeles, California. (Photo by Mark Sennet/Getty Images) 3. Steven Spielberg holds his Oscar after winning Best Director for his movie *Saving Private Ryan* during the 71st Academy Awards, March 21, 1999, at the Dorothy Chandler Pavilion in Los Angeles, CA. AFP PHOTO/Timothy A. CLARY. 4. Steven Spielberg attends The Prelude to the Paris Games 2024 on July 25, 2024 in Paris, France. (Photo by Marc Piasecki/WireImage)

Collect the Little People, BIG DREAMS™ series:

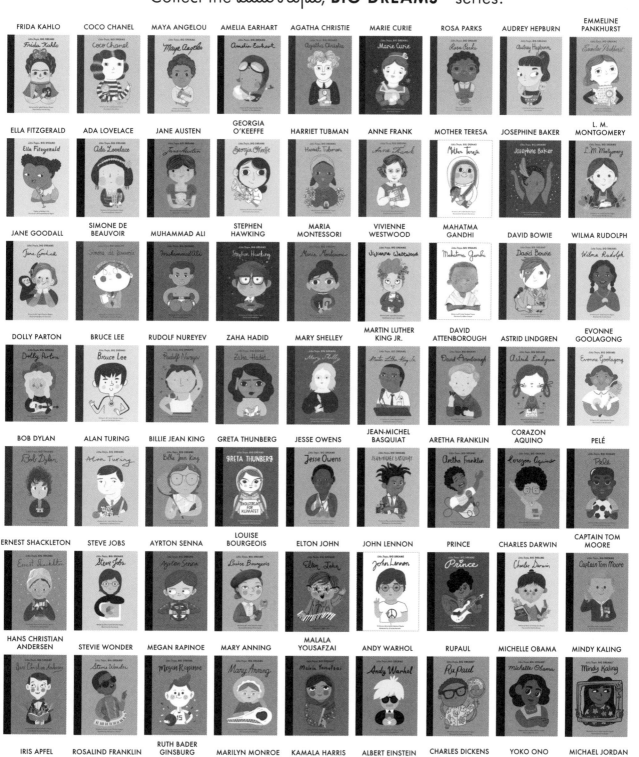

FRIDA KAHLO · COCO CHANEL · MAYA ANGELOU · AMELIA EARHART · AGATHA CHRISTIE · MARIE CURIE · ROSA PARKS · AUDREY HEPBURN · EMMELINE PANKHURST

ELLA FITZGERALD · ADA LOVELACE · JANE AUSTEN · GEORGIA O'KEEFFE · HARRIET TUBMAN · ANNE FRANK · MOTHER TERESA · JOSEPHINE BAKER · L. M. MONTGOMERY

JANE GOODALL · SIMONE DE BEAUVOIR · MUHAMMAD ALI · STEPHEN HAWKING · MARIA MONTESSORI · VIVIENNE WESTWOOD · MAHATMA GANDHI · DAVID BOWIE · WILMA RUDOLPH

DOLLY PARTON · BRUCE LEE · RUDOLF NUREYEV · ZAHA HADID · MARY SHELLEY · MARTIN LUTHER KING JR. · DAVID ATTENBOROUGH · ASTRID LINDGREN · EVONNE GOOLAGONG

BOB DYLAN · ALAN TURING · BILLIE JEAN KING · GRETA THUNBERG · JESSE OWENS · JEAN-MICHEL BASQUIAT · ARETHA FRANKLIN · CORAZON AQUINO · PELÉ

ERNEST SHACKLETON · STEVE JOBS · AYRTON SENNA · LOUISE BOURGEOIS · ELTON JOHN · JOHN LENNON · PRINCE · CHARLES DARWIN · CAPTAIN TOM MOORE

HANS CHRISTIAN ANDERSEN · STEVIE WONDER · MEGAN RAPINOE · MARY ANNING · MALALA YOUSAFZAI · ANDY WARHOL · RUPAUL · MICHELLE OBAMA · MINDY KALING

IRIS APFEL · ROSALIND FRANKLIN · RUTH BADER GINSBURG · MARILYN MONROE · KAMALA HARRIS · ALBERT EINSTEIN · CHARLES DICKENS · YOKO ONO · MICHAEL JORDAN